Pack

ANIMAL TRACKS IN FULL LIFE SIZE

Ed Gray
Illustrated by DeCourcy L. Taylor, Jr.

STACKPOLE BOOKS

Copyright © 2003 by Ed Gray
Illustrations copyright © 2003 by DeCourcy L. Taylor, Jr.
Published by
STACKPOLE BOOKS
5067 Ritter Road
Mechanicsburg, PA 17055
www.stackpolebooks.com

Printed in U.S.A.
10 9 8 7 6 5 4
First edition
Cover design by Caroline Stover

All animal drawings also show a house cat or a human in order to indicate relative size.

0 11557 02818 8

WEASEL

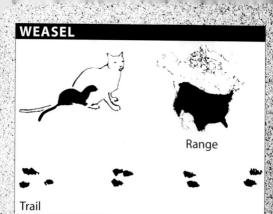

Range

Trail

MINK

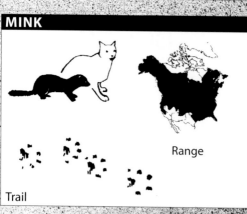

Range

Trail

MARTEN

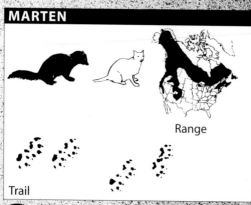

Range

Trail

2

Fore

Hind

Fore

3

SQUIRREL

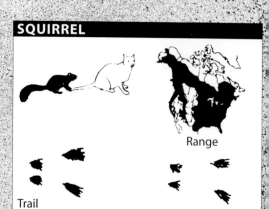

Range

Trail

WOODCHUCK

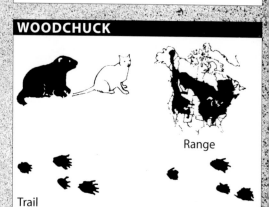

Range

Trail

MUSKRAT

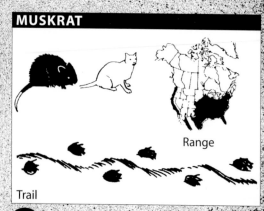

Range

Trail

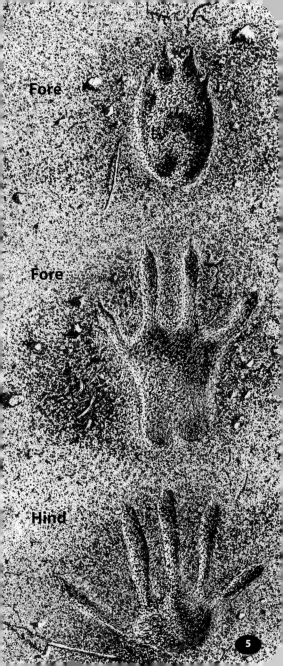

OPPOSUM

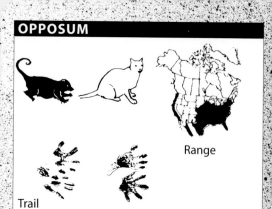

Trail

Range

RACCOON

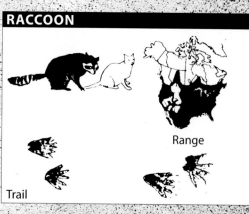

Trail

Range

SKUNK

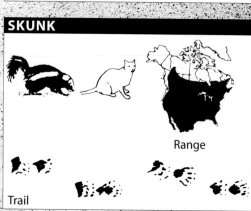

Trail

Range

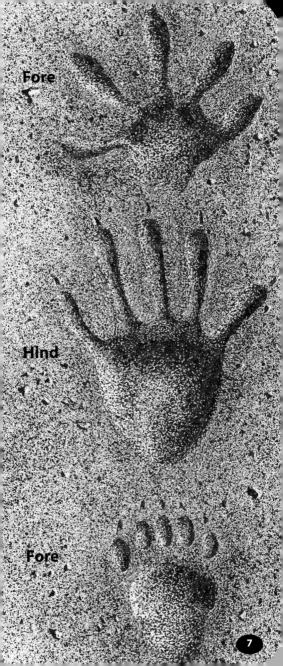

Fore

Hind

Fore

7

FISHER

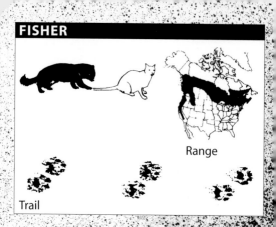

Range

Trail

OTTER

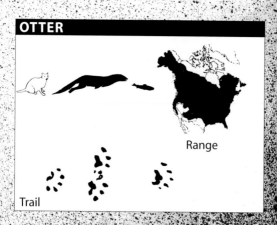

Range

Trail

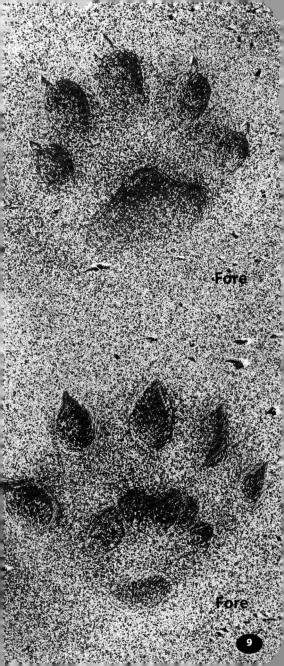

Fore

Fore

9

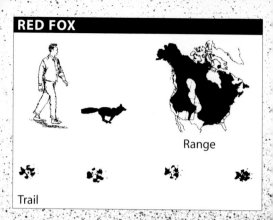

RED FOX

Range

Trail

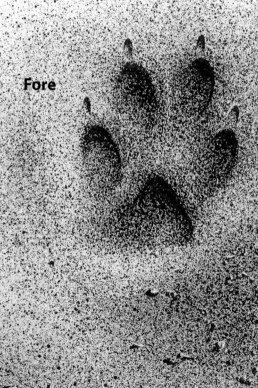

Fore

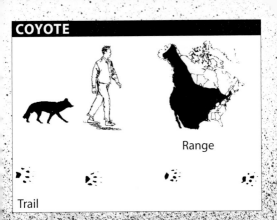

COYOTE

Range

Trail

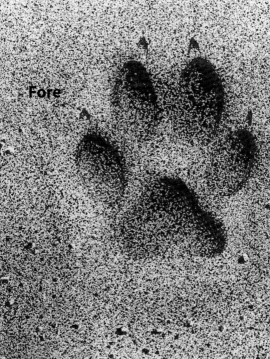

Fore

BADGER

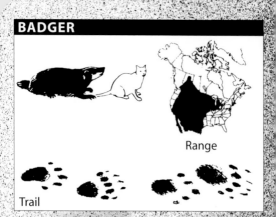

Range

Trail

WOLVERINE

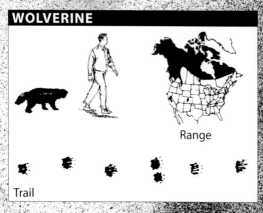

Range

Trail

12

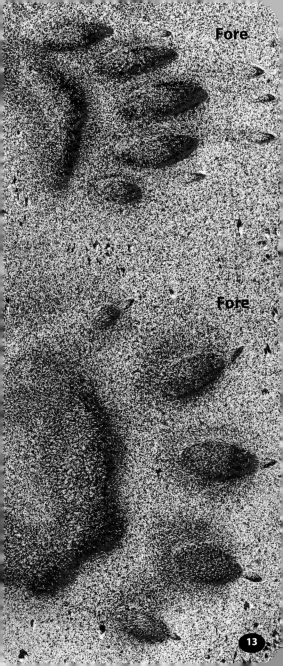

Fore

Fore

13

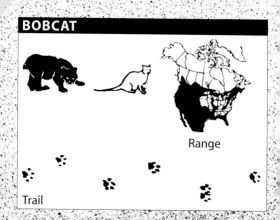

BOBCAT

Range

Trail

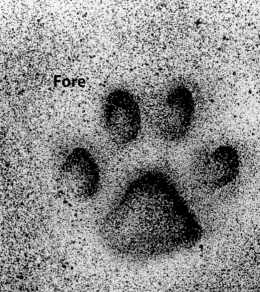

Fore

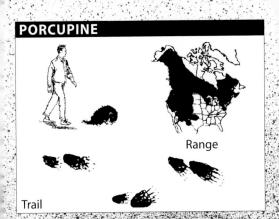

PORCUPINE

Range

Trail

Hind

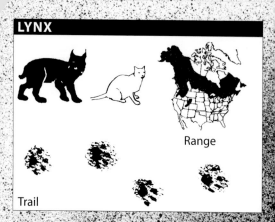

LYNX

Range

Trail

Fore

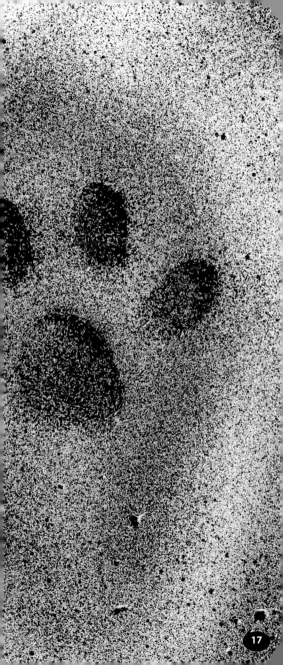

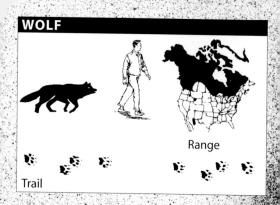

WOLF

Range

Trail

Fore

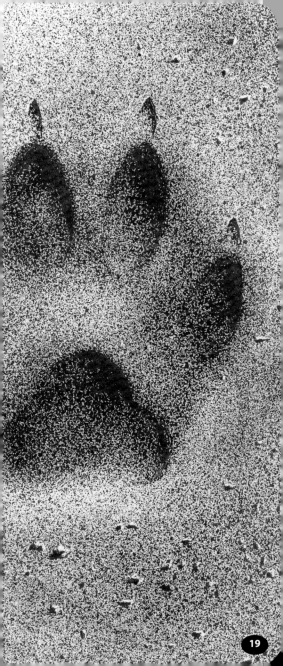

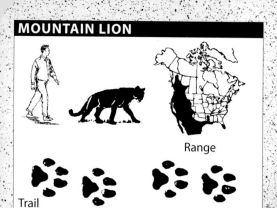

MOUNTAIN LION

Range

Trail

Fore

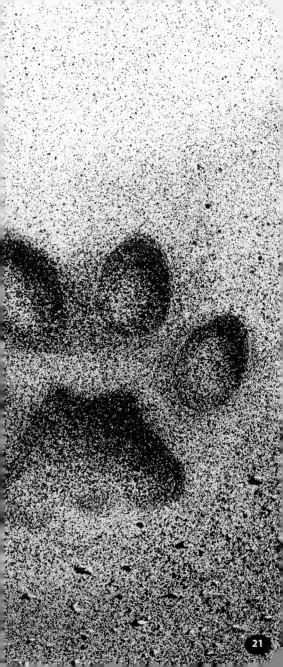

COTTONTAIL RABBIT

Trail

Range

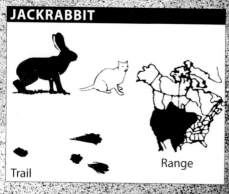

JACKRABBIT

Trail

Range

SNOWSHOE HARE

Trail

Range

Hind

Hind

Hind

23

Hind

BEAVER

Trail

Range

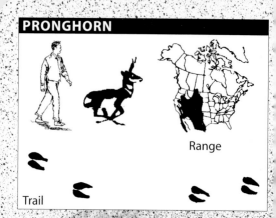

PRONGHORN

Range

Trail

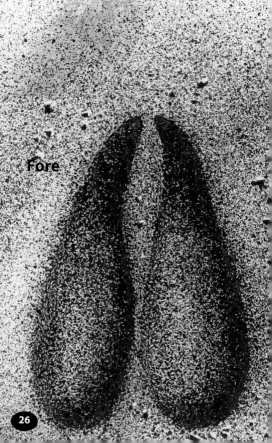

Fore

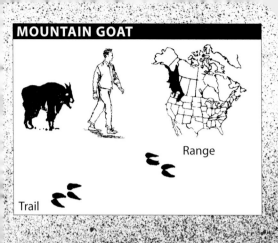

MOUNTAIN GOAT

Range

Trail

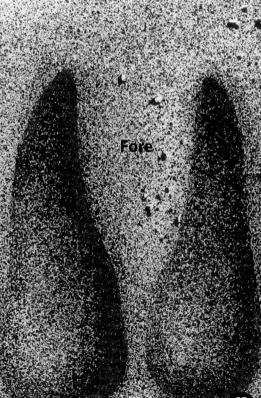

Fore

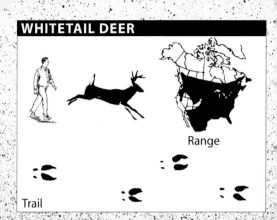

WHITETAIL DEER

Range

Trail

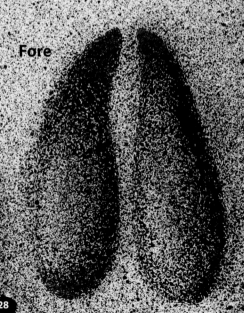

Fore

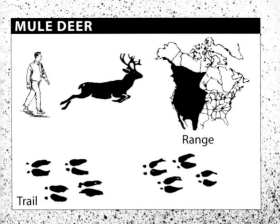

MULE DEER

Range

Trail

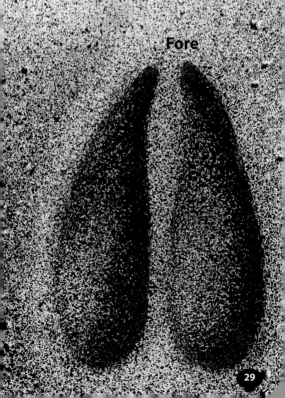

Fore

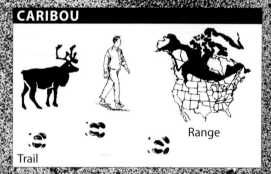

CARIBOU

Range

Trail

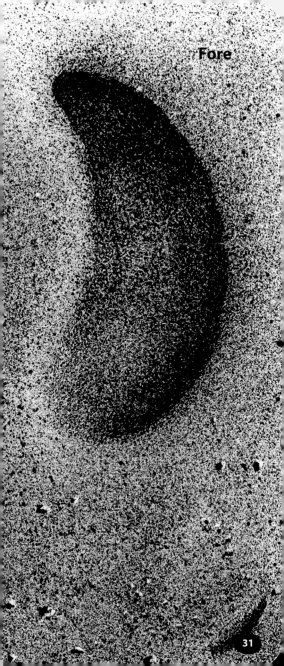

Fore

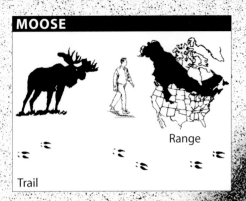

MOOSE

Range

Trail

Fore

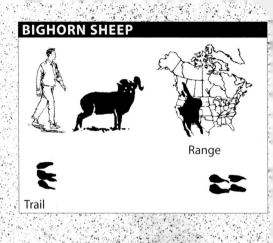

BIGHORN SHEEP

Range

Trail

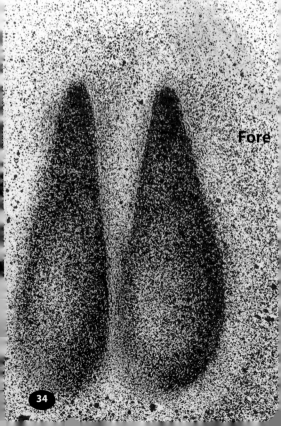

Fore

Fore

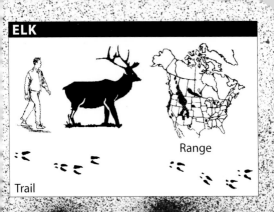

ELK

Trail

Range

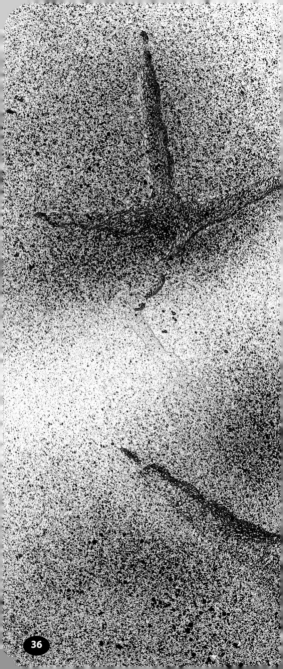

GRIZZLY BEAR

Range

Trail

Hind

BLACK BEAR

Range

Trail

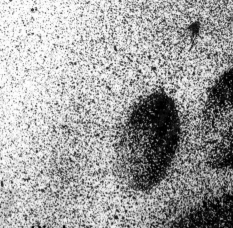

Hind

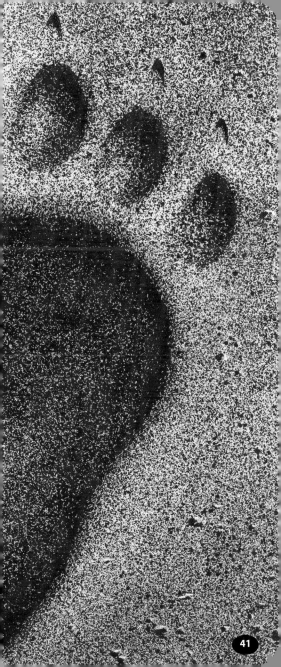

ABOUT THE AUTHORS

Ed Gray is the co-author, with Benjamin Kilham, of *Among the Bears*. He founded *Gray's Sporting Journal* with his wife, Rebecca, in 1975, and was its editor for sixteen years. He has been a contributing editor to *Esquire Sportsman* and *Sports Afield*, and writes fiction and essays from his home in New Hampshire.

DeCourcy L. Taylor, Jr. has been a painter and a sculptor for over forty years. He originated the design of *Gray's Sporting Journal*, and was its art director for sixteen years. He is currently designer and art director of the *Atlantic Salmon Journal*, the magazine published by the Atlantic Salmon Federation, and lives in Texas.